A GUID

The Do's

OF

House & Cottage Conversion

Written & Illustrated by

Hugh Lander

Foreword by

ALEC CLIFTON–TAYLOR

M.A., F.S.A., Hon.F.R.I.B.A.

author of THE PATTERN OF ENGLISH BUILDING,
SIX ENGLISH TOWNS (B.B.C.), etc.

CONTENTS

FOREWORD

From the very fact that you have troubled to buy, or at least to read, this booklet, I assume that you are concerned about the appearance of your house or cottage.

Well, you could hardly find a better adviser than Hugh Lander. His observations abound not only in wisdom but in good taste, reinforced by sound historical knowledge and a concern for what is practical too.

It may not always be possible to obtain today the materials with which an old house was built. But there are good substitutes and there are poor ones. Be very careful.

Apart from the materials, both of walls and of roofs, it is in the windows that the worst mistakes are usually made. There are a lot of very commonplace windows available now, with which the good appearance of an old house can be practically ruined. Great attention is given here to window design, and rightly so. If you follow Mr Lander's advice you will be all right.

I commend this booklet with great pleasure.

ALEC CLIFTON-TAYLOR

INTRODUCTION

This booklet has been produced because the writer is alarmed to see how few old, stone-built cottages, houses and other small buildings retain their identity after work has been carried out upon them.

The aim therefore is to provide a clear set of guide lines, with appropriate illustrations, for those involved in converting, renovating or extending such buildings.

For maximum clarity, the booklet has been written in the form of a very precise set of Do's and Don'ts for each part of the building being converted.

It is the architectural quality of the ordinary houses, shops and pubs which give a small town or village its distinctive appeal. The country rectories, farm houses, isolated barns, abandoned mills, chapels and crofts lend flavour to the rural landscape.

If the renovation or conversion of these old buildings is not sensitively undertaken, then just those qualities which give them their attraction will be lost, and our heritage diminished.

AGE DESTROYED

Many buildings are so thoroughly 'straightened up' and important features, such as doors and windows, so unsuitably replaced, that all semblance of age is destroyed.

It has become a relatively common practice for owners to demolish all but a few feet of the walls of a building. Onto this pathetic vestige of the original is brutally grafted a modern dwelling – totally at odds with its country surroundings. Had the planning applicant sought permission to construct a *new* house on the site, he would have courted instant rejection.

In many instances, hideous alterations may be made without any legal obligation to obtain planning permission at all.

Even when the intention is *genuinely* one of restoration, and the owner has set about the work in good faith, the results can still be lamentable.

WRONG POINTING

It may be that he has employed the wrong kind of pointing for the stonework, or introduced an unsuitable bow window of the sort favoured by other 'improvers' in his neighbourhood. He may have flattened out the pitch of the roof, or replaced double-hung sash windows with stock casements. The list is almost endless. A Sunday afternoon drive in any area will quickly provide more than enough evidence for this gloomy view.

Much of what this booklet proposes has become recognised *in theory* by architects, planners and conservation bodies in many parts of the country. Yet even these, though sometimes scathing in their criticism, are exceedingly cautious in spelling out details of what they would actually recommend.

Many writers on these topics are so keen to avoid accusations of personal bias or dogma that they will favour carefully ambiguous generalisations. For instance, they will insist that an old building should remain 'in character' or 'in keeping', but will not give definite guidance about what should actually be done.

VICTORIAN REPLACEMENTS

Local authorities – if they can be pinned down at all – have a distressing tendency to clutch at bad precedents when advising planning permission applicants.

"No, we can't allow those modern windows," they tell the bewildered owner. "You must put back the kind it's got already." The fact that these may be ugly Victorian replacements of eighteenth century originals will not worry them in the least.

One of the greatest fears of architects, planners and other members of the cognoscenti is to be thought guilty of any kind of 'faking'. They will allow a totally unsuitable modern extension to an old building, provided that it is, in their parlance "an honest expression of the best contemporary design", or is "in tune with the ambience and aspirations of our times". These protestations often disguise the sociologist or politician manqué, rather than a person whose primary concern is for beauty.

UGLY PASTICHES

Followers of this persuasion, and there are many, often appear unable to distinguish the difference between imaginative and informed use of period detail, and the ugly pastiches which give proper use of these devices an undeservedly bad name. Had former ages subscribed to the popular modern views on using classical detail, matters would have stopped short at the Parthenon.

We would have been deprived of all Roman architecture, the villas of Palladio, and eighteenth century delights like Mereworth and Chiswick, not to mention Carlton House Terrace, or even St George's Hall, Liverpool.

The professionals of the building world and technically-minded amateurs may, on the whole, be trusted to see that repairs and extensions are carried out in a competent manner. What, alas, they manifestly cannot do (in many cases) is make the houses they are renovating still look old when they have finished with them.

Although this booklet is based on a knowledge of sound building procedure, it is not intended to supply detailed technical instruction. There are numerous excellent publications available which deal with every practical aspect of construction and repair work. The glossary, however, should assist readers in planning and researching the work and talking with professionals.

* * * * * * *

This booklet attempts to provide a coherent list of suggestions for those who would value help in preserving the aesthetic qualities of stone vernacular buildings.

In the last event you are free to accept or reject them as you please, but I hope at least these three aims will have been achieved:

1. To have engaged your interest in the subtle exterior details of house conversion, which can make or break the final result.
2. To make some small contribution towards checking the number of houses which are being badly restored or converted.
3. To show that the choice is essentially one between beauty and ugliness.

Britain is still well supplied with lovely old houses and cottages in endless variety, but the stock is dwindling. It is not enough to save these buildings from actual demolition. We must also save them from the cruel doctoring which makes them hard and vulgar parodies of their former selves.

RETAINING CHARACTER

Most people know, or think they know, what is meant by the phrase 'retaining the character' of an old building. Whether or not they know *how* to achieve this purpose is more problematical.

The most obtuse individual will be vaguely aware of an old building's visual merits, but what *his* eye will accept as suitable in the way of restoration and conversion work may make others grind their teeth and avert their gaze.

The idea is to help readers in a straightforward way to avoid losing the character of an old house. No attempt has been made to blur issues or hedge bets. Some will think this arrogance and others will see it as honesty.

Here, it is worth considering the qualities of an old house which are loosely described by the general term 'character':

a) Architectural period
b) Appearance of age
c) Individuality

Architectural Period

The features which denote period in a house, such as window and door design, roof pitch, eaves detail, scale and proportion, are more *obviously* important to take into account than those which display age or individuality.

As a general rule, you may do worse than preserve the period by ensuring that any new work is carried out in the same manner and with similar materials to those originally used.

It should be remembered that it is not only the front elevation of a house or cottage which matters. You should also exercise the same care and attention in repairing or replacing elements of the side walls or in dealing with the back of a building.

Each contributes to the character in its own context and will be visible to somebody *some* of the time and, perhaps, to someone else *all* of the time.

How often one admires the front of a modest Georgian town house, only to step into the garden at the back to be confronted by a hotch-potch of hideous replacement windows, strangely projecting additions and ugly finishes.

Appearance of Age

Retaining an appearance of age is, in many ways, more difficult and controversial. Obviously, the crazy dip in the roof ridge, the moss grown tiles and leaning chimneys contribute greatly to a sense of age. They may however be ineffective, or at worst, structurally dangerous.

Yet all that is old is not necessarily beautiful, or indeed characteristic of the building. For example, a pair of Victorian bays may have been added to the facade of an early 18th C. rectory. These will be old in themselves (say 130 years), but from an aesthetic point of view may have ruined the building.

The question here is whether or not later additions detract from a building's merits, or add to them. The problem demands individual judgement, bearing in mind that the ways in which people see buildings can change from one generation to another.

The best rule to apply is: if it is aesthetically pleasing, not dangerous and does not actually threaten the building's future (e.g. dry rot), leave it alone. Thus, if the ridge is stable and not leaking, the tiles do not let in the rain and the chimney is not liable to collapse, let them be.

What if you *have* to replace or repair? This is where opinions about 'honesty' vary. Some people say you should use old materials to blend in; others advocate using the same type of materials in a new state, letting them show up until they weather naturally. A third view is that you may disguise new materials artificially by tricks of the trade. Whichever course you take you will not go far wrong provided that you have employed genuine materials in the right architectural style.

What should you do about the loss of age implicit in replacing an undulating roof ridge with a new straight one? Personally, I think that if structural necessity demands a new ridge, you might just as well make it straight, as it no doubt was when the house was first built.

The technical difficulties and increased cost of faking ancient faults of this kind more or less preclude the practice. The new chimney may be built of similar stone in the same manner, but it had better not lean over!

The ethics of faking have already been mentioned and provide another whole field of discussion. They beg the questions: "what is faking?", "what is copying?" and "what is original design in a traditional idiom?"

I believe that to reconstruct an old roof with all its dips and undulations would be faking. To scrape random bits off a new floor joist with a spoke shave and fire No. 6 bird shot at it to simulate woodworm is faking.

Ethically, faking may be bad; aesthetically, it may largely depend upon whether or not your fake is successful. Usually, it will fail dismally. Here, we enter the eternal argument about the aesthetic value of the portait by Van Dyck which suddenly turns out to be Bloggs c. 1934. Alas, we have no space to pursue it.

Individuality

The individuality of a house is the most difficult quality to analyse. Abstracts like charm, eccentricity and atmosphere are awkward to tab down and, if it were not for fear of losing them, it is doubtful if one would wish to do so anyway.

They are of great importance, however, and it would be a pity to remove some appealing, dotty feature in the interests of efficiency and too slavish an adherence to authentic detail.

Setting also contributes much to individuality, and many a nice old building is robbed of its distinction when surrounded with tarmac, old trees truncated and everything tidied up beyond endurance. Old houses should be mellow. Efforts to imbue them with suburban rectitude will leave the owner (one hopes) with a sense of unaccountable dissatisfaction.

No matter how much money you spend, and work you carry out on converting, repairing or extending an old building, you have failed if it no longer looks and feels old when you have finished.

THE 'ROUGH' AND THE 'SMOOTH'

Throughout this booklet, reference is made to 'rough' and 'smooth' houses. The former category includes most old cottages, many farmhouses and the majority of buildings not designed for dwelling purposes. Their stonework is often of random rubble. Their facades are frequently unbalanced and their interiors make few pretences to elegance.

The 'smooth' group may be said to include the smaller houses of merchants and professional men, rectories and manors which all subscribe to a mainly classical form of design. They will have balanced and evenly spaced architectural features and may contain interior panelling, mouldings, fine staircases and fireplaces. The house on the back cover is 'smooth', while that in illustration No. 1 is 'rough'. The house on the front cover is somewhere between the two.

BEFORE & AFTER

Fig 1 (above) *A semi-derelict 19th C. croft-farmhouse, early part on the right, in the state known as 'ripe for conversion'. Only the walls and some principal roofing timbers can be saved.*

Fig 2 (below) *The same building after repair and conversion work is finished. The old doorway has been unblocked to form a new entrance. The original roof lines have been retained. Stonework has been exposed and pointed back, where practicable.The roof would have been nicer in real slate; but the building is probably not of sufficient quality to merit the high cost. Note, however, that the asbestos/cement substitutes have faded and weathered, giving the roof a fairly unobtrusive appearance.*

The windows have been replaced with 12-pane double-hung sashes, having horns in keeping with the period of the left hand part of the building. The front door is a plain ledged-and-braced affair.

The original front door of the newer and larger part of the house has been converted to a window, allowing a large three window sitting room on the ground floor. This has slightly upset the balance of the facade; but, since the building is of the 'rough' variety and already asymmetrical, it is not especially tiresome to the eye.

MIGHT HAVE BEEN

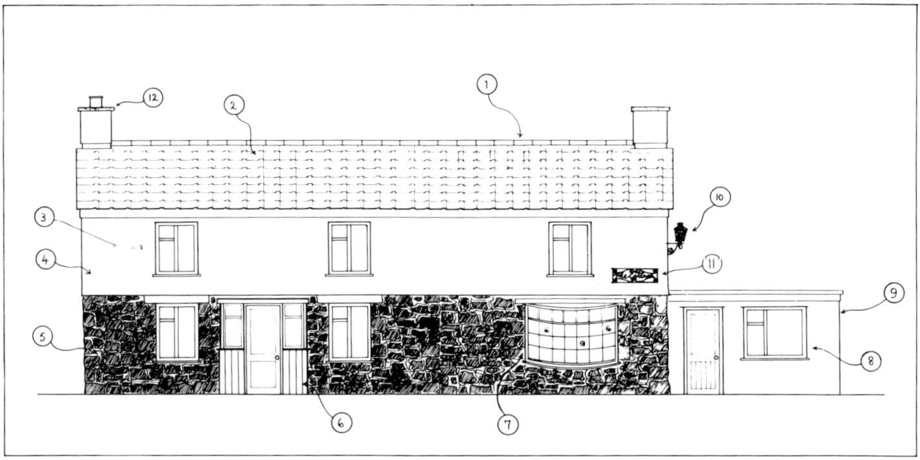

Fig 3

How NOT to restore the farmhouse in Figs. 1 and 2. It is no exaggeration to say that such buildings usually stand an odds-on chance of ending up very like this drawing.

Twelve popular and damaging features of modernisation are shown:

1. *Right hand roof line has been raised to make a single, uniform and age-disguising ridge.*
2. *Modern concrete interlocking tiles destroy any sense of age.*
3. *Stock joinery windows of totally unsuitable design.*
4. *Hard, smooth rendering carried down to a bell-cast conceals concrete block rebuild of the upper floor. Effect is entirely modern.*
5. *Stonework outlined in ugly ribbon or strap pointing. Look on to illustration no. 39 for a close-up of this.*
6. *Modern, useful, but absolutely unsuitable porch.*
7. *Fake bow window with top opening lights and sham bull's eye panes.*
8. *Hideous picture window.*
9. *Ugly, flat-roofed extension with half-glazed door of modern pattern.*
10. *Modern wrought-iron lantern of incongruous design.*
11. *Suburban looking name sign of bent metal strips.*
12. *Flat concrete chimney capping.*

WINDOWS

DON'TS

1. Don't use modern designs for old houses. **Figs 18-28**
2. Don't repeat ugly Victorian, or later replacements, in older buildings. **Figs 4-6**
3. Don't use stock bow windows in the wrong setting. **Figs 3 & 25**
4. Don't use picture windows. **Figs 3, 26 & 27**
5. Don't use frosted, obscured or textured glass.
6. Don't on any account use a different and *modern* design for additional windows. **Figs 18-28**
7. Don't use fake bull's eye panes *at any time* in any form of window.
8. Don't, on any account, put u.P.V.C. windows in old buildings. They will destroy the mellow sense of age, whatever patterns of imitation glazing bars the manufacturers have employed. *(See also page 18).*

DO'S

1. Do use small-paned double hung sash windows where suitable (usually late 17th century onwards). **Figs 8,9,10**
2. Do use nine pane casements rather than six pane ones **(Fig 7)** These will probably be suitable for small windows in new extensions, or for small new window openings in 18th and 19th century houses. Types of use envisaged · landings, passages, tiny bedrooms and lavatories. **Fig 17**
3. Do use Cornish or Yorkshire horizontal sliding sashes where suitable. **Figs 12 & 13**
4. Do use white paint on wooden windows as a general rule (see Paint and Colour section).
5. Do try and retain any old 'crown' glass panes available (see glossary).

Note

In houses which pre-date the late 17th century where wooden or stone mullions with leaded paned casements were in use. **(Figs 15 & 16)** , existing original windows should be faithfully copied, or expert professional advice obtained. It may be necessary when replacing early sash windows to use individually ordered glazing bars of a thicker section than that normally used by specialist joineries. For houses of any quality, supply joinery with templates or samples of sash mouldings.

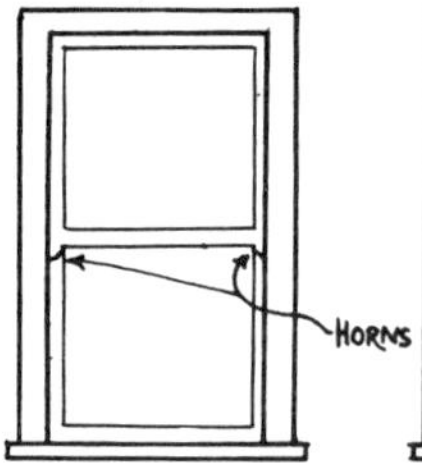

Fig 4

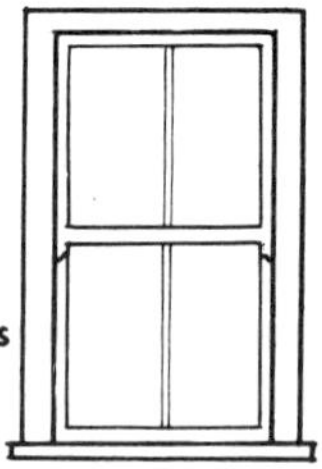

Fig 5

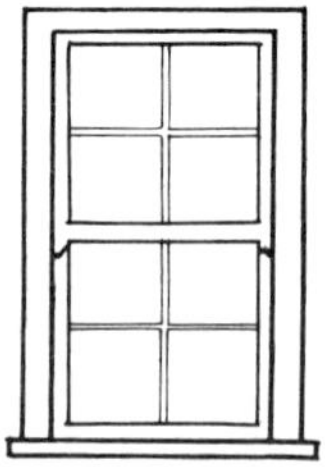

Fig 6

Victorian houses may CORRECTLY have sash windows like these (with horns); but the 12-paned variety is incomparably better. Precedents for 12 panes abound to a surprisingly late date.

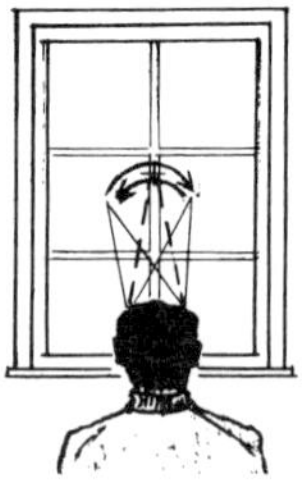

Fig 7 *The 'gunsight' effect of paired window panes. The eye, confused by the duality, may finally focus on the central glazing bar.*

WINDOWS

DO USE.....

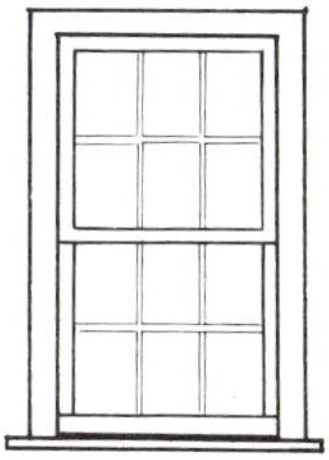

Fig 8 *The delightful 12-pane double-hung sash window. It may be employed (with minor variations of detailing) for the majority of houses dated 1690-1850, (no horns - see glossary)*

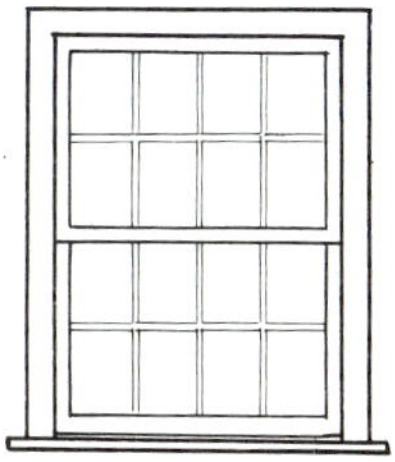

Fig 9· *The excellent 16-pane double-hung sash is more usually found in late 18th C. and early 19th C. houses. Lends itself to wider window openings. (No horns)*

Fig 10 *The double-hung sash with 'Gothic' tracery glazing bars may be seen in buildings c.1770 to c. 1840. Very attractive with early 19th C. stucco.*

Fig 11 *The cruciform window with stone or timber mullion and transom has numerous rectangular leaded panes. The type found in many late 17th C. buildings.*

Fig 12

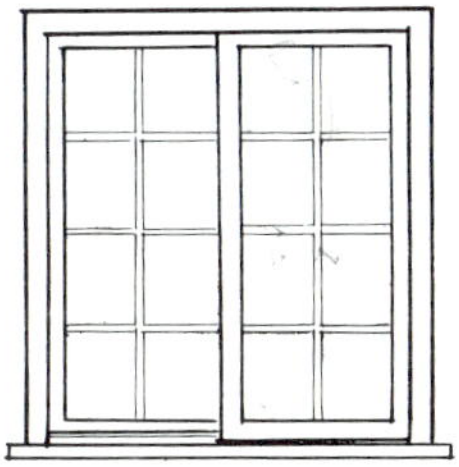

Fig 13

The Yorkshire or Cornish horizontal sliding sash window is often found in the more cottagey type of building. Has character and dates from early 18th C.

Fig 14 *The paired fixed light and opening casement (preferably of 9 or 12 panes) was quite often used in late 18th C. and early 19th C.*

Fig 15 *Stone mullioned window with hood mould and diamond leaded panes. Making these is highly specialised work and may apply to 16th C. or early 17th C. building. (seek advice).*

Fig 16 *Stone mullioned windows like this, with a straight cornice and rectangular leaded panes may be required for a 17th C. house. (seek advice).*

Fig 17 *The useful and and, on the whole, pleasing 9-paned casement. Good for staircases, passages, cottage gables and other oddments which do not merit a double-hung sash.*

WINDOWS

DON'T USE.....

Fig 18 *DON'T use the modern stock casement window with mullion, transom and top opening light.*

Fig 19 *DON'T use this modern form of the 17th C. cruciform.*

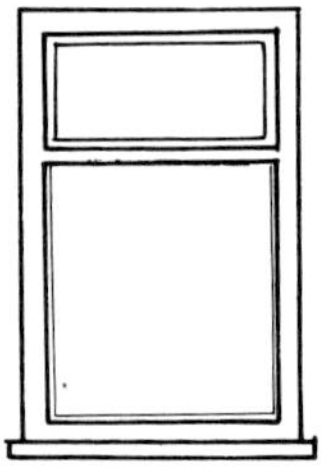

Fig 20 *DON'T use this either, even with glazing bars.*

Fig 21 *DON'T use this.*

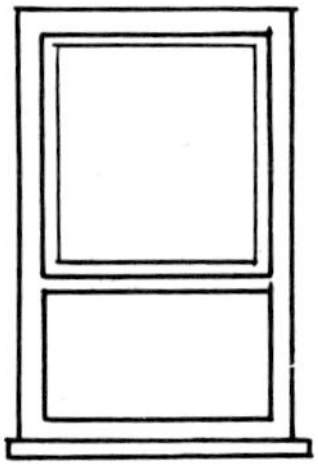

Fig 22 *AVOID this also.*

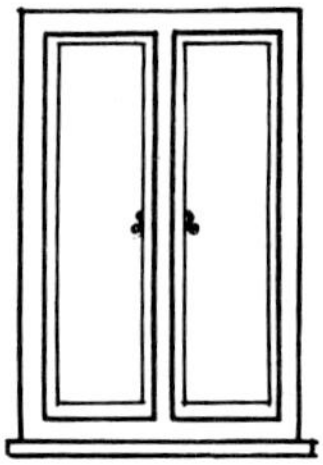

Fig 23 *AVOID this.*

Fig 24
Resolutely REJECT versions of this.

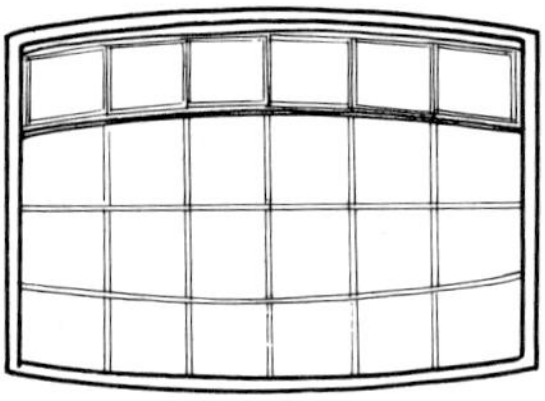

Fig 25 *AVOID, at all times, modern versions of the bow window. If a bow window is imperative, have it made after seeking specialist advice on authentic detailing.*

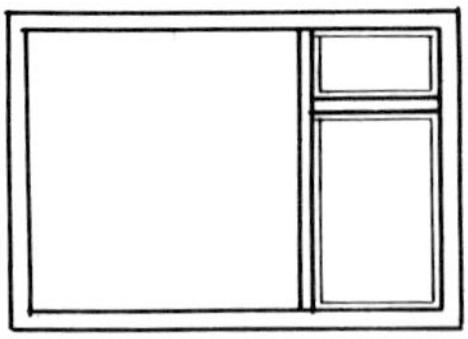

Figs 26 & 27
The picture window in two of its many forms. NEVER use it in connection with an old house.

Fig 28 *The eye-confusing casement with paired panes should be AVOIDED, although it may sometimes be correct.*

WALLS

DON'TS

1. Don't use ugly forms of pointing for stonework. **Figs 39,41,43,44**
2. Don't use hard, flat renderings.
3. Don't use pebble dash, spatter dash or Tyrolean finishes. **Figs 38 & 40**
4. Don't demolish old walls and rebuild unless structurally unavoidable. **Fig 29**
5. Don't replace or add to stonework in materials of different tone or texture i.e. insert an exposed concrete lintel over a window in an old stone wall.
6. Don't straighten up and modernise leaning or undulating walls which are structurally safe. **Fig 29**
7. Don't use vertical crazy paving to face walls. **Fig 45**
8. Don't use composition concrete tiles for cladding.
9. Don't use asbestos cement slates for vertical cladding.
10. Don't use waney-edged weather boarding on houses. **Fig 42**

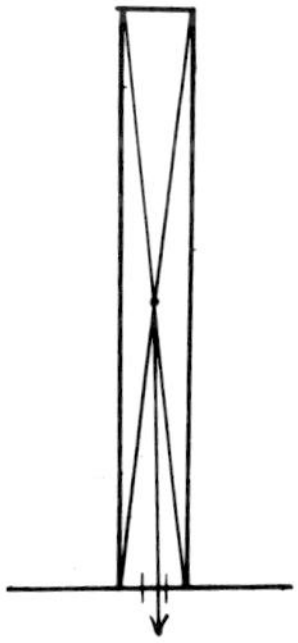

Fig 29 *The middle-third rule allows that a leaning wall may be safe provided that: a) It is not subject to further settlement, new and excessive loads or disturbances; b) a notional line suspended from its centre of gravity hang within the middle third of its thickness. (seek advice).*

DO'S

1. Do point walls in 1:1:6 cement, lime and sand mortar, or even weaker mixes than this.
2. Do use coarse, sharp sand of the right colour, and brush the pointing to texture it before it sets. **Fig 31**
3. Do rake out joints between stones to at least 1" depth and keep new pointing well back from the face of the stone. **Fig 31**
4. Do render walls with weak cement/lime/sand plaster mixes.
5. Do use genuine rough cast (where regionally appropriate) but only after obtaining expert advice.
6. Do use wood float finishes to give a rough texture. **Fig 34**
7. Do retain the natural undulations of the stonework when plastering 'rough' stone buildings (this does not apply to old stucco buildings).
8. Do expose old stonework whenever possible, rather than plastering it over. (Note: some late 18th century and early 19th century rubble stone buildings were intended for stucco plastering when they were built). **Fig 30**
9. Do use textured paints and Snowcem etc., but only where original stonework cannot reasonably be rescued with good pointing. **Fig 31**
10. Do disguise new concrete blockwork with natural stone; slate cladding; sawn feather-edged weather boarding; or tile hanging. **Figs 32 & 35**

WALLS

Fig 30 *GOOD example of an early 19th C. house which is designed to be faced with a hard, smooth stucco finish, in keeping with the classical detail of the pilasters.*

Fig 31 *GOOD pointing. The mortar is textured, of suitable colour and is kept well back from the surface of the stones.*

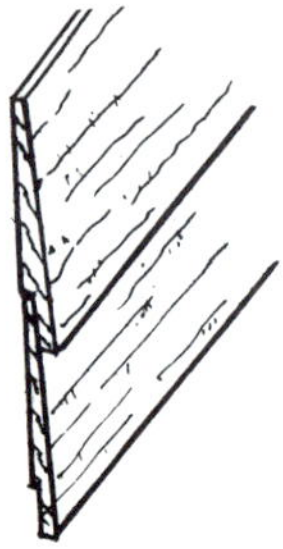

Fig 32 *Feather-edged weather boarding.*

Fig 33 *GOOD finishes for rough stone walls include this form of 'whitewash' effect, where the stones are clearly defined.*

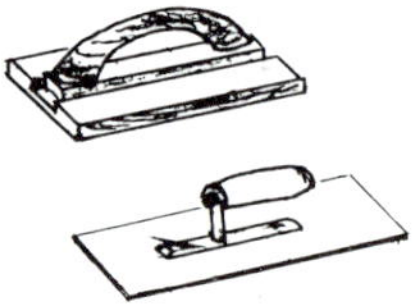

Fig 34 *Above: a wood float for texturing plaster. Below: a steel trowel for laying-on plaster and smooth finishes in general.*

Fig 35 *GOOD slate hanging like this will often enhance an old building or disguise a new addition.*

PLASTER FINISHES TO AVOID

Fig 36 *AVOID quaint textured finishes like this. They look modern and out of keeping.*

Fig 37 *AVOID eccentric forms of texturing when rendering an old building. This one looks like measles.*

Fig 38 *AVOID spatterdash. It is not totally objectional, but other finishes are better.*

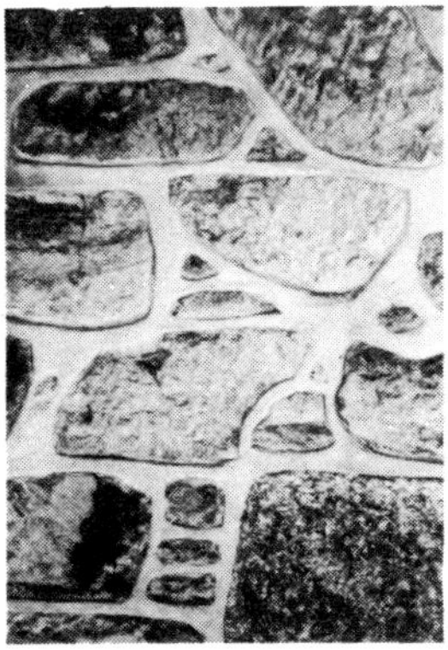

Fig 39 *BAD ribbon or strap pointing. It stands out from the face of the stones and creates a coarse and obtrusive visual effect. Technically, it also tends to trap moisture, directing it back into the joints.*

Fig 40 *AVOID using pebble-dash on old houses. It fails to please. Paint helps to disguise it.*

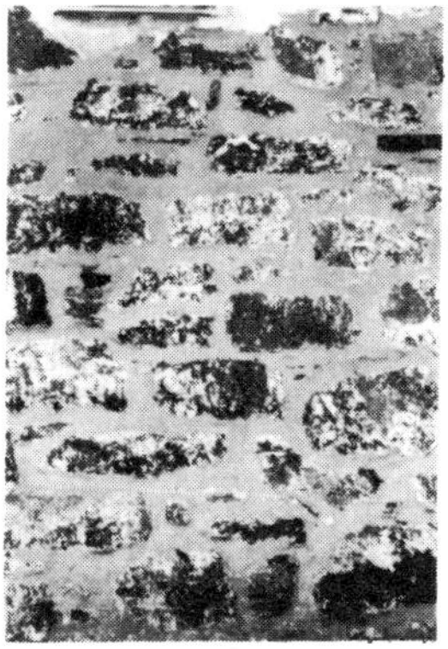

Fig 41 *BAD pointing which has been smeared over the face of the stone-work. It is of poor colour and looks messy and amateur.*

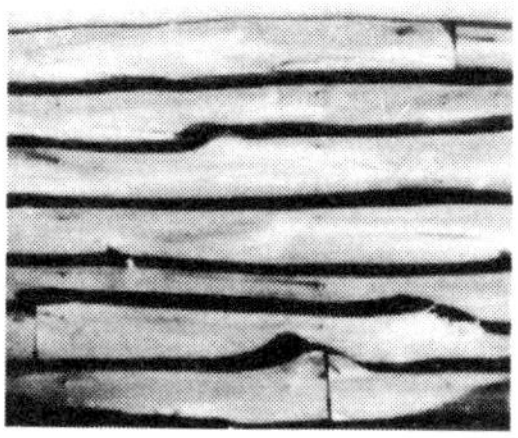

Fig 42 *AVOID this waney-edged weather boarding when cladding parts of old buildings. It can look rather 'Hollywood'.*

Fig 43 *BAD pointing. Here the mortar has been smeared over the face of the stones and then given a spurious and ugly finish by the creation of projecting 'tucks'.*

Fig 44 *BAD pointing. The stones have been pointed and then emphasised in white, giving the wall a hard, ugly and distracting appearance.*

Fig 45 *BAD use of genuine stone in the form of a vertical crazy paving, used as a facing. The effect is modern, busy and ugly.*

ROOFS

DON'TS

1. Don't flatten out the roof slope (the pitch). **Fig 47**
2. Don't use concrete interlocking tiles. **Fig 49**
3. Don't bring a new uniformity into your roof lines when improving or extending a building. **Fig 46**
4. Don't replace a nice old roof unless it is structurally essential.
5. Don't rebuild old chimneys unless structurally essential, or introduce new chimneys in modern styles. **Fig 50**
6. Don't introduce dormer windows of modern style and proportions. **Fig 48**
7. Don't demolish or modernise old dormers in old roofs. **Fig 48**

DO'S

1. Do choose harmonious materials such as real slate, real stone slates, thatching, weathered plain tiles, weathered pantiles, 'Roman' tiles. These last three may be real old ones or new ones artificially weathered in appearance by applying a cowdung solution; or it may be possible to obtain new ones of subtle colour.
   *Asbestos slates **(Fig 2)** may sometimes be used as a second best, and they do weather successfully to some extent. Note that all these roof coverings must be chosen according to regional styles.
2. Do retain varied roof lines. **Fig 46**
3. Do use dormer windows to improve lighting and ventilation of top floor rooms, if it will avoid raising the original roof line. **Fig 47**
4. Do sometimes use dormer windows of correct proportions and design to introduce character to an extension of an old building.

Note

Real Welsh slate eventually weathers in a variety of greys, blues and violets, whereas asbestos-cement slates merely become toned down by the effect of uneven fading. Cornish 'Delabole' slate is probably one of the most attractive to be found anywhere.

Fig 46 *If you start like this....*

DON'T end up with this....

Aim for something more like this.

ROOFS

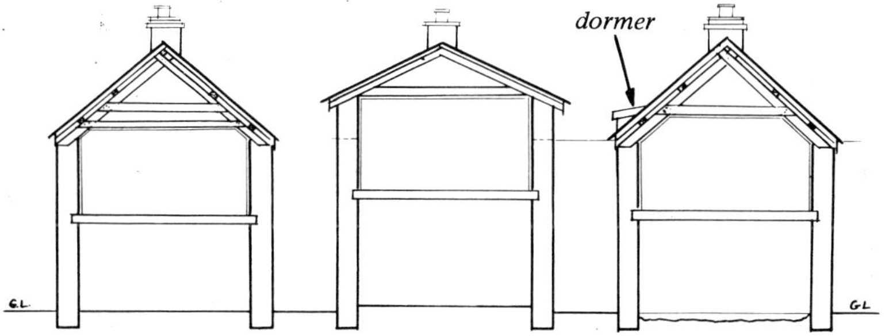

Fig 47 *A* *B* *C*

A typical cottage roof structure (A) is all too often flattened out to accommodate raising the eaves line (B), so increasing the ceiling height upstairs and down. The better solution (C) gains space by excavating the ground floor and forming a 'camp' ceiling upstairs. The window is raised by dormering. The roof pitch is unchanged.

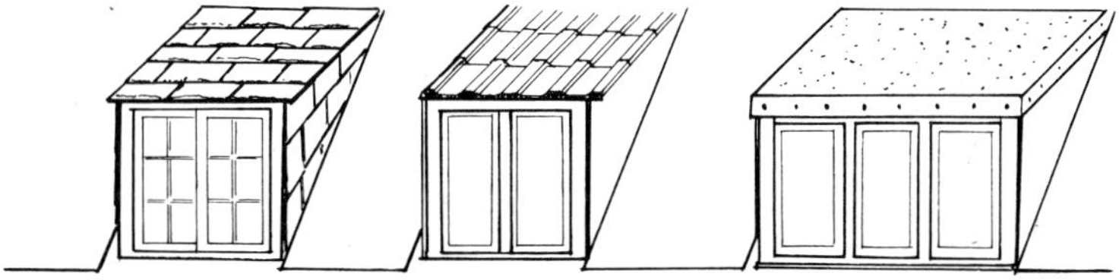

Fig 48
DON'T let an old dormer like this.... TURN INTO this.... or WORSE STILL, this.

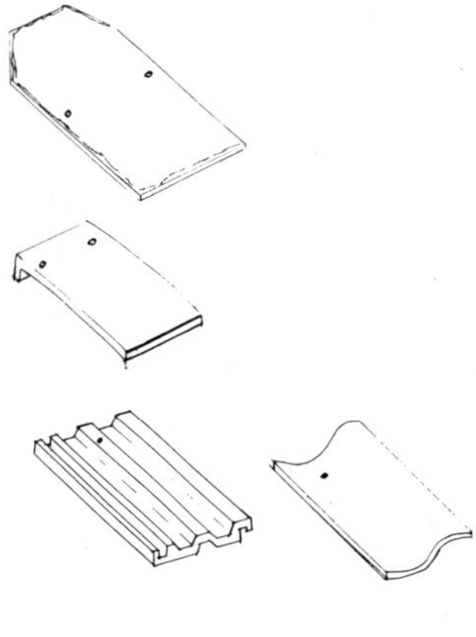

Fig 49
Top: ordinary roofing slate. Below: plain tile with nib. Bottom left: AVOID the many versions of modern interlocking tiles. Bottom right: pantile.

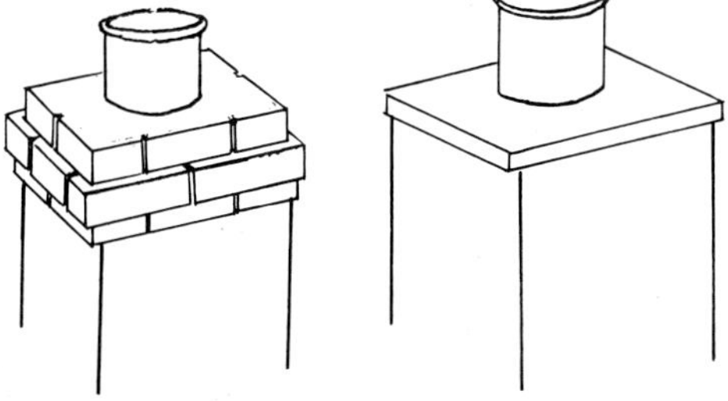

Fig 50
Chimneys like that, left, with corbelled courses of brickwork, should on NO ACCOUNT be repaired or replaced in the form shown, right. Here, the chimney has been smooth rendered and topped with a precast concrete capping – a totally modern device.

PORCHES & DOOR HOODS

DON'TS

1. Don't put modern glass porches on old houses **(Fig 3)**. The obvious physical attractions of having a 'hot box' on the front of your house should never outweigh the damage it will do to its appearance.
2. Don't have flat roofs on enclosed porches, unless faithfully copying a suitable period design.
3. Don't use vulgar and inappropriate mock Georgian pediments, cornices, pilasters and pillars. **Fig 52**
4. Don't use a porch at all unless you can get it exactly right.

DO'S

1. Do make quite certain any porch enhances your building rather than detracts from it.
2. Do use properly pointed stone porches where appropriate **(Fig 54)**. Also trellis porches, slate-hung porches or weather-boarded porches may be in keeping in some cases. **Fig 55**
3. Do use slate slabs on brackets for door hoods **(Fig 56)**. Slated or tiled pitched roofs may also be used. **Figs 58 & 59**
4. Do use *genuine* variations of Georgian designs, with hoods, cornices or pediments if in keeping. **Figs 51 & 53**

Note

You will first have to decide whether you are adding a minimal front door shelter in the form of a door hood to keep the rain off visitors' heads, or an enclosed porch to be used as an additional weather break, and for other purposes. The trellis porch is, of course, a compromise between the two. It cannot be stressed too much that great care and finesse is required if you are to add a successful door hood or porch to an old house.

DOORS & WINDOWS

One of the most pervasive threats to old buildings during the 1980's has been the introduction of u.P.V.C. replacement doors and windows. Despite the manufacturers' efforts to design some of them in ways which refer to the wooden originals, they never succeed in looking anything but fakes. They provide a certain recipe for ruining an old house or cottage.

Their finish looks plastic. The methods of opening, in the case of windows, is scarcely ever authentic. The 'glazing bars' are nothing like genuine ones and, although some types of window adopt a similar number and distribution of panes, they still have a relentlessly modernising effect. Any local planning authority which allows them in a *listed building* should be ashamed of its philistine decision.

If, one day, somebody devises a u.P.V.C. window which is truly indistinguishable from the real thing, I shall be happy to reconsider these strictures.

Avoid all u.P.V.C. Doors and Windows

PORCHES & DOOR HOODS

Fig 51 *Typical vernacular Georgian detailing of a doorway, with fanlight, triangular pediment and broken entablature.*

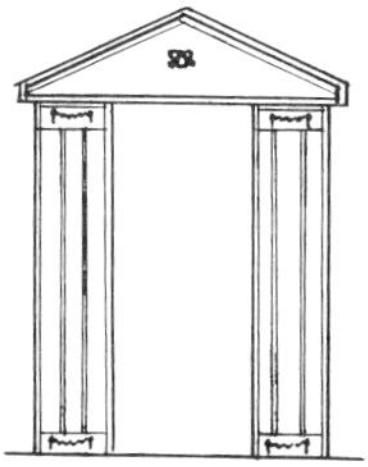

Fig 52 *AVOID modern pastiches of classical doorway detailing. Study the orders of architecture.*

Fig 53 *A good, plain six-panel door within a doorway with segmental stone arch, simple cornice and cap mouldings. Very late 18th C. or early 19th C.*

Fig 54 *One of the best solutions is a simple stone porch with a pitched roof.*

Fig 55 *A pretty trellis-work porch of the kind used in the first half of the 19th C.*

Fig 56 *A good simple device for a door hood, consisting of a slab of slate resting on plain wrought-iron brackets.*

Fig 57 *This heavy granite slab on corbels would provide an effective hood for a 'rough' cottage.*

Fig 58 *A solid and not unpleasing modern porch for an old cottage.*

Fig 59 *Another robust porch with whitewashed stone and a slate roof. Would do for many a 'rough' stone building.*

DOORS

DON'TS

1. In general, don't use full length glass doors as front doors. **Figs 61 & 62**
2. Don't use iron-studded doors as front doors unless there is good evidence to show that this was local practice at the date in question. If you do have this evidence, get the door made to a properly researched specification. **Figs 65 & 66**
3. Don't use any form of frosted or obscured glass in a door. It may have practical advantages, but normally looks very out of place.
4. Don't (as a rule) use stock doors from joinery works catalogues, although there *are* a few patterns available which may be suitable.
5. Don't use metal up-and-over doors for garages. They always strike a modern note.
6. Don't fit new u.P.V.C. doors in old buildings, whatever the practical temptations. They are bound to fail however hard the manufacturers have tried to make them look like old ones. (See pictures on page 18).

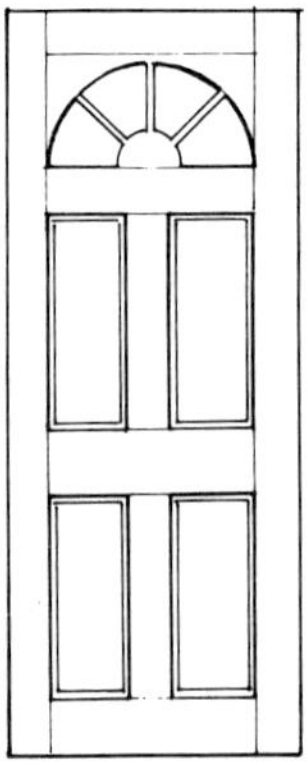

DO'S

1. Do use doors which are in character with the building. See note below.
2. Do use suitable door hinges and door furniture. **Figs 72 & 73**
3. Do use panelled doors, ledged and braced doors or stable doors. **Figs 68 to 71 inc.**
4. Do pay strict attention to the details of panel mouldings, width of boards, and overall proportions of any glass panes, and of the door itself.

Note: The doors on page 21 (opposite) have, for the sake of convenience, been drawn with narrow, sentry box proportions, but the old ones are normally much wider than this; and look the better for it.

In all cases the type of door will vary according to the style and age of the building. In some instances you will be looking for a formal, panelled variety. In another (for a rough stone cottage) a ledged and braced plank door may be more suitable. Early buildings, i.e. 17th century and earlier, may demand doors of hardwood construction and require specialised period design. On such occasions, seek expert advice and carry out research.

AVOID the all too available "doll's house" door, with its crude imitation fanlight, where the top two panels should really be. Doors like this are totally out of keeping with any old building. True Georgian fanlights occupy the space above a transom, which divides the glazed part of the door opening from the panelled door itself.

DOORS

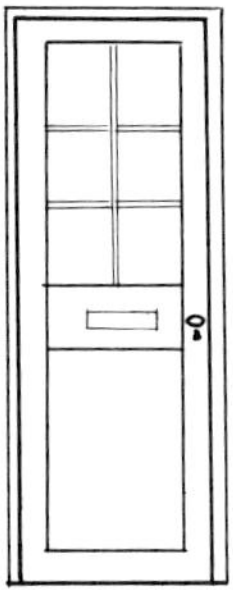

Fig 60

Fig 61

A VOID all these

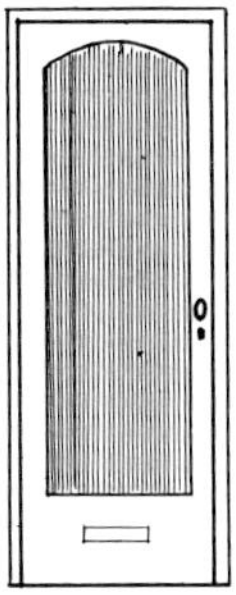

Fig 62

Fig 63

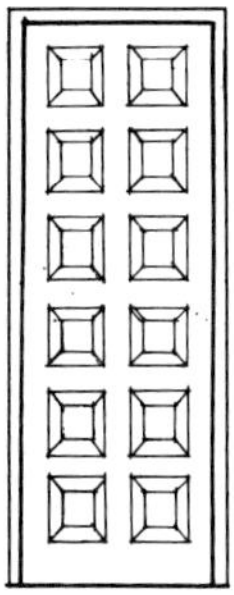

Fig 64 *Although something rather like this was used in the 18th C., it is generally best avoided.*

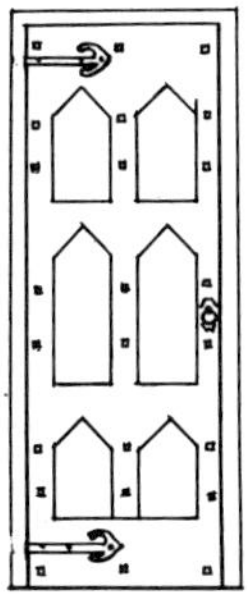

Fig 65

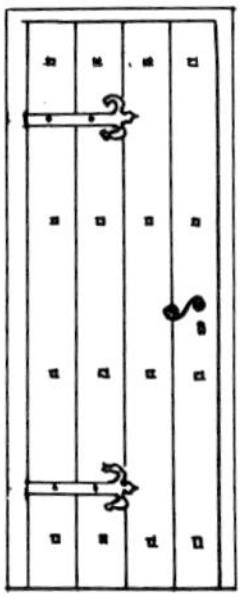

Fig 66

A VOID all 'olde worlde' detailing.

Fig 67 *This glazed stable door is wrongly proportioned, the top part being far too deep.*

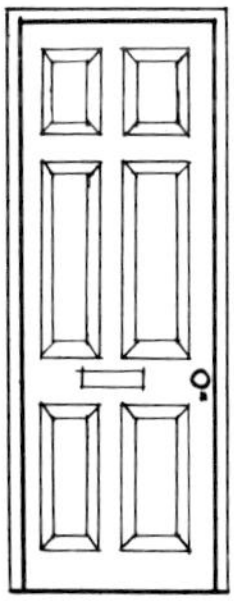

Fig 68 *GOOD all purpose 6-panel door, ideal for most 'smooth' houses. (Study panel mouldings before ordering)*

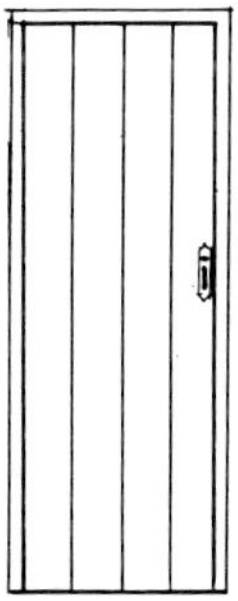

Fig 69 *Simple ledged and braced door. Excellent for all kinds of 'rough' houses, inside and out.*

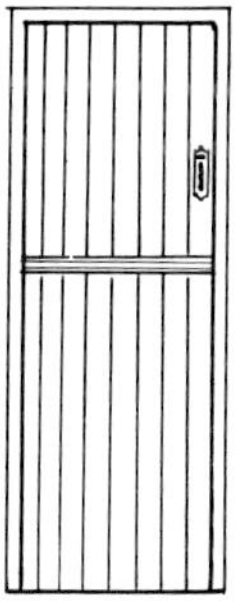

Fig 70 *GOOD, simple, stable door for cottages and converted mills, etc.*

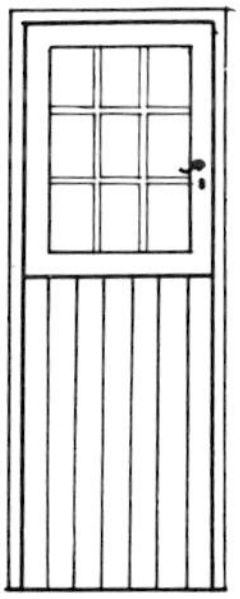

Fig 71 *The part-glazed version of Fig. 70. Note the 9-pane design and proportioning.*

EXTENSIONS

DON'TS

1. Don't add flat-roofed extensions. They always look modern. **Fig 3**
2. Don't use unsympathetic modern wall finishes for extensions. If in doubt try to match the original materials from which the house was built.
3. Don't allow the extension to spoil the scale and character of the original building. **Fig 3**
4. Don't allow the extension to dominate by its newness and size. i.e. observe scale.
5. Don't use a different style of window in the extension to that of the old windows in the original house. **Fig 3**
6. Don't use concrete composition interlocking tiles for the roof. **Fig 49**
7. Don't use modern door designs just because it is a new piece of building. **Figs 60 to 66**
8. Don't use hard, sharp and straight wall finishes, unless the original building is of formal stucco construction. **Fig 30**

DO'S

1. Do make the extension harmonise with the original house.
2. Do, if possible, use materials which will weather and tone with the original.
3. Do use properly pointed stone for walls **(Fig 31)**, soft plaster with a wood float finish, weather boarding, slate hanging or tile hanging.

Note

The general principle to be observed when adding an extension is to make it harmonise and look as though it has always been there. The materials used should, if possible, be already weathered, and if not they should be such that they will blend in as quickly as possible. It may be argued that some extensions in a modern idiom are successful, but examples are so rare that it is safer to discount them.

PAINT & COLOUR

DON'TS

1. Don't, as a general rule, paint window frames and glazing bars any colour but white.
2. Don't use varnish, or any gloss finish sealer, on exterior woodwork which is intended to have a natural wood appearance.
3. Don't as a general rule paint walls of *rural* properties in strong, bright colours.
4. Don't paint the pointing of stone or brickwork.
5. Don't paint lines on the pointing between bricks or stones to emphasise the courses. **Fig 44**
6. Don't think the colour of a garage or outhouse door does not matter.
7. If you live in a terrace house don't use colours which vie with those of your neighbours.

DO'S

1. Do use white paint for window frames, glazing bars, and in most instances, for fascia boards. Occasionally there may be a case for using black, dark blue, brown or green on some parts of windows. Green glazing bars were not uncommon in American 18th century houses. Very occasionally, frames may be painted black to advantage, when adjoining walls are white.
2. Do paint plaster or timber mouldings, coves and cornices white, as a general rule.
3. Do treat natural softwoods with an oil preparation. It is argued that hardwoods do not benefit from treatment.
4. Do paint walls of *rural* properties in gentle colours, which will tone in with the landscape, e.g. buff, sand, grey, certain greens and some terra cottas.
5. Do reserve the brighter colours (blues, yellows, pinks, etc.) for properties by the sea or water or in more urban settings. Sometimes the wall of a fisherman's cottage can be effectively painted black or tarred.
6. Do paint up-and-over metal garage doors in a suitable disguising colour, but preferably avoid using this kind of door at all.
7. Do take the opportunity of painting the woodwork of outbuildings in a unified scheme.
8. If you live in a terrace, do use a colour which blends rather than clashes with that of your neighbours. In a stuccoed crescent or terrace, which has been built as an architectural unity, it is often best to collaborate with your neighbours in choosing a suitable colour for use throughout.

DO'S continued

9. As a rule, do paint exterior ironwork black.
10. If it is necessary to pick out formal detail of ironwork in gold, do use proper gold leaf, rather than gold paint, if possible.
11. Do consider painting cast iron guttering and down pipes in a colour which merges rather than contrasts with the walls. Sometimes guttering will have to match the fascia rather than the wall.
12. Do take pains to preserve and repair any old lead down pipes and hopper heads.

IRONWORK & ORNAMENT

DON'TS

1. Don't use fake ornamental strap hinges on exterior doors. They will make the building look newer rather than older. **Figs 65 & 66**
2. Don't apply or use fake 'medieval' iron studs to the outside of doors. **Figs 65 & 66**
3. Don't use *bad* imitations of old iron door knockers, door knobs and letter boxes.
4. Never use chrome, imitation gilt or plastic house numbers on front doors.
5. Don't apply modern wrought-iron house name signs to your walls or gates. **Fig 3**
6. Don't use 'rustic' wooden house signs with the name applied in poker-work paint or plastic lettering. **Fig 75**
7. Don't use flimsy and unconvincing wrought iron gates, porch brackets, lanterns or plant holders. Good, old, wrought ironwork has substance and the scrollwork, if any, has subtle variations in thickness. **Figs 74 & 77**
8. Don't use bad modern imitations of old lanterns or coach lamps for outside lighting. **Fig 3**
9. Don't set up bad copies of Victorian cast iron street lamps to light your garden path or forecourt.
10. Don't mock-up artificial well heads where no well exists, or fabricate an unconvincing imitation of a well head above a genuine well.
11. Don't apply fake shutters of unsuitable design to your windows, especially those which cannot in fact be closed.

DO'S

1. Do hang ledged-and-braced doors on simple business-like iron strap hinges (note: for constructional and security reasons these will usually be inside). **Fig 73**
2. Do use *good* handwrought replicas of early ornamental strap hinges on plank doors of houses sufficiently old to merit them.
3. Do use good solid brass door knockers, plates, knobs and other door furniture for 18th and 19th century houses. These should be designed in the true spirit of the period and should never be lacquered.
4. Do use 'Norfolk' or 'Suffolk' thumb latches on simple plank cottage doors. **Fig 72**
5. Do use solid iron door knockers and door knobs of suitable design, finish and texture.
6. Do be very sparing and careful about the use of electrified conversions of genuinely old coach lamps for outside use. They can look bogus.
7. Do use, for house names: a) brass plates with incised lettering. b) wooden rectangular plaques with name painted in simple script, or some other, and reasonably restrained characters.
   c) a painted sign in similarly restrained lettering on the gate or door itself.
   d) unlacquered brass lettering of good design and proportion screwed to the wood of the door or gate.
8. Do use well-designed brass house numbers, or paint suitably designed numerals on the wood.

IRONWORK & ORNAMENT

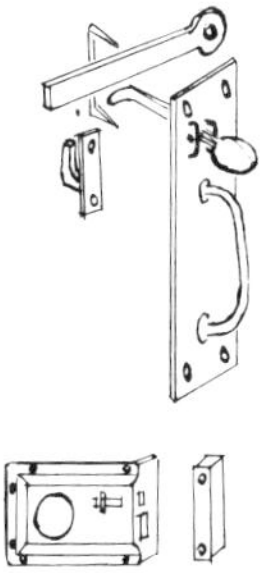

Fig 72
Above: Thumb-latch of roughly Norfolk or Suffolk type. This is the standard black-japanned iron-mongers variety. Perfectly suitable in 'rough' cottages, although hand-made variations may be preferred.
Below: Ironmongers standard rim-latch, which, with brass knob is an ideal piece of furniture for simple cottage doors. Rim-lock on the same lines for exterior doors is not burglar proof.

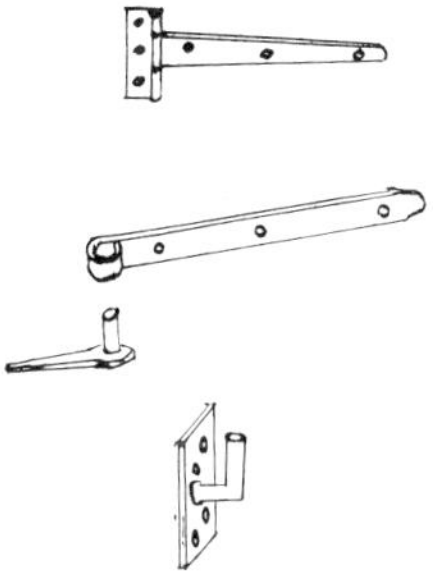

Fig 73
Top: 'T' hinge. A good standby for vernacular work.
Below: Mild steel strap hinge or cross garnet, with two types of gudgeon pin. Good simple device for cottage gates and doors.

Fig 74 *Good ironwork of spirited but robust design - late 18th C.*

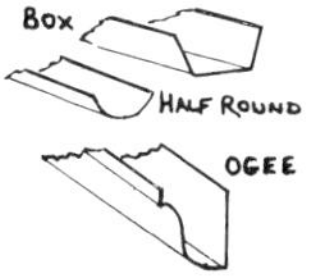

Fig 77a *Three commonly available types of gutter. See 'GUTTERS', page 28.*

Fig 75
House signs like this can look suburban on old buildings, especially when varnished.

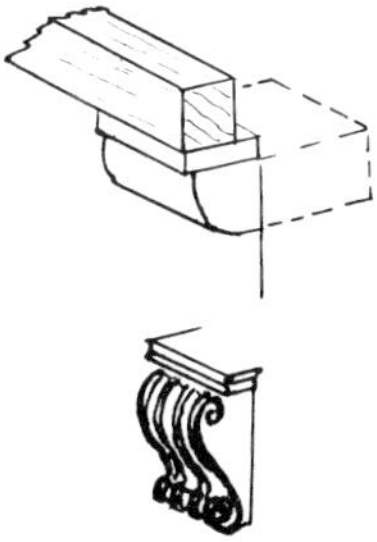

Fig 76 *Above: Stone corbel carrying a timber wall plate. Below: Scrolled and fluted ancone or console bracket.*

Fig 77 *Uniform looking 'wrought-iron' bent from stock metal sections, does not enhance an old house.*

IRONWORK & ORNAMENT

DO'S continued

9. Do, for the support of lanterns, plant-holders, door hoods and so on, faithfully copy good old ironwork designs, or seek expert advice. Do use simple softwood brackets for the support of door hoods, or in some cases, stone or moulded plaster consoles. **Fig 76**
10. Do design well heads for existing wells in the most strictly functional manner, using, as far as possible, old materials and following good examples of old ones in the area. Some old ones *are*, of course, elaborate; and a really good modern craftsman may do this kind of thing to advantage.
11. Do design shutters which can be closed satisfactorily against the weather and are of suitable weight to serve their purpose. These will normally be of tongued and grooved boards, cross battened. Occasionally, they may be of louvred design. The latter are more often found on early 19th century town houses.

Fig 78 This satisfying 18th C. town house, with its rusticated granite quoins, string course and brick facing to the upper floors, has been skilfully restored, retaining a quite pleasing widened Victorian entrance.

The replacements of the 19th C. plaster consoles under the door cornice have been hand carved in pine by the owner, who has also designed a new door and doorcase to fit the opening. The door furniture is good modern brass. The railings are new.

The decision of the local authority to retain the Victorian features of the facade has been echoed in the horns used for the new 16-pane windows.

The alternative - my choice and, incidentally, the owner's - would have been to pull the downstairs windows back into line, reinstate the lower string course, and research a suitable Georgian doorcase and door. It must be conceded however, that the final result is attractive.

LANDSCAPE & SETTING

DON'TS

1. Don't cut down trees in the vicinity of the house unless it is absolutely imperative for the most urgent reasons of safety.
2. Don't savagely pollard healthy mature trees.
3. Don't strip well established creepers and flowering shrubs from walls, unless the building is so exceptional that it *must* be revealed.
4. Don't lay any kind of path or hard standing in concrete where it can readily be seen. Use instead: toppings, bricks, cobbles, flagstones, gravel or beaten earth. Tarmac of the right composition once it has really weathered will look all right for a hard standing, but is usually second best.
5. Don't build outhouses, garages, or other buildings on the sky line, or in prominent positions, unless they are to be specially designed features worthy of the original house.
6. As a general rule, don't impose paths on the garden by merely laying out a logical plan on paper. This tends to look too rigid. Some more formal gardens, of course, do demand this approach.
7. Don't construct such features as ornamental pools using a concrete or mortar finish.
8. Don't lay paving for paths or terraces in such a way that the slabs are pointed in between with mortar.
9. Don't imagine that lawns and flower beds *must* be shaped like kidney dishes. This is merely a passing fashion. Some of the loveliest herbaceous borders in the land run straight as a die.

DO'S

1. Do lop trees sparingly if they must be cut back; and do it in such a way as to retain the shape and balance.
2. Do divide the garden into interlinking areas, with their own character and purpose, using fences, hedges, pergolas and walls. They will make the garden look bigger, not smaller.
3. Do create a vista framing a landscape which appeals to you.
4. Do make paths and terraces from such materials as old bricks, slate or stone slabs. If you use crazy paving, lay it in sand, not mortar, and encourage sweet smelling herbs to grow between the stones.
5. Do make full use of the natural lie of the land to form lawns, terraces, glades and parterres.
6. Do use pergolas, archways, trellises, avenues of trees, tubs, cisterns, urns, fountains, cascades, old, or really good reproduction statuary, sundials, arbours, loggias and summer houses (of special design).
7. Do plant traditional herbaceous borders if you can cope with the upkeep.
8. Do line ornamental pools with real stone or other genuine materials.
9. Do use box, yew, escalonia and lonicera hedges. Be sparing of privet and laurels.
10. Do use sawn feather-edge board fences, park railings, posts-and-rails.

LANDSCAPE & SETTING

DON'TS continued

10. Don't place your vegetable patch or kitchen garden in an unscreened position, unless you are determined to have a REAL cottage garden, where the roses rub shoulders with the runner beans. It is a genuine, but not always attractive practice.
11. As a rule, don't demolish old garden walls if they can be repaired and pointed, as described in the section on walls.

DO'S continued

11. Do let pathways establish themselves through usage, and then lay down the paving or other material afterwards.

Note
When employing firms of 'tree surgeons' make sure first that they are not merely 'tree butchers'.

GUTTERS

Eaves gutters pose a number of aesthetic problems for those repairing old houses. An important factor is that many earlier cottages did not have guttering in the first place. Often, the ones you see are of 19th C. or even 20th C. origin. Thatched buildings do not need guttering at all.

'Smooth' houses may have lead lined gutters hidden behind parapet walls or cornices, disgorging rainwater into lead bucket heads and downpipes. Sometimes, buildings had wooden eaves gutters, attached in the position of the fascia board. They were often of built-up construction in more or less elaborate moulded forms, and were lead lined.

In the 19th C. cast-iron gutters, of both ogee and half-round section, were in widespread use. Today, however, we have the following main types to choose from:- cast-iron ogee (double curve) or half-round; aluminium ogee section; plastic in square (box) and half-round sections; galvanised iron and asbestos cement types, both in half-round. (See Fig 77a, page 25)

Local authority building inspectors *do* like to see a nice set of gutters draining every possible area of roof. What should we select? Cast-iron ogees are probably the most pleasing. There is not much to choose between half-round forms of cast-iron and plastic, except as far as finish and colour are concerned. Cast-iron *must* be painted and plastic *may* be, if it appears too alarming.

Plastic square section is meant to look better on old buildings; but I always think it is a bit uneasy. Aluminium ogee is light for fixing and of good shape, but the colour and finish would suggest painting. This rather wastes the attraction of being rustproof. On a cost basis, plastic wins by a mile; but try to resist making money the chief criterion.

CONCLUSION

At this point, having hammered the unfortunate reader with a formidable list of prohibitions and advice, it is worth recalling your attention to some rather more generalised matters.

The first of these is to remind you that converting houses should be fun. You should enjoy the discoveries, the research, the physical conquest over obdurate materials, and the sense of achievement when beauty at last transcends ugliness and decay.

Please do not think that it is my intention to stifle imagination and creative ideas. Should you faithfully adhere to every single principle set down here the opportunities for indulging your personal taste and inspiration will still remain endless.

If you have never lived in an old house before, it is worth remembering that it is likely to be more expensive in many respects than a new one. It is a responsibility both in the practical sense, as well as in the aesthetic. No matter how thorough you have been in your works of restoration, there will always be hidden faults which may eventually confront you with some costly or time-consuming repairs.

However, an old building will return you dividends which far outweigh any of these considerations of duty and expense. It will delight the eye, sooth the spirit, reward the touch and enhance every simple aspect of daily life.

Sometimes it will come about that you realise you have made a thundering mistake in the way in which you have chosen to carry out a change or addition to your house or cottage. It happens to everybody - but don't be too timid or proud to do anything about it. You will, alas, become quickly accustomed to an infelicity. Show true grit and tear out the offending work, rather than learn to live with it.

Never allow yourself to be ham-strung by the Building Regulations. More often than not, a proper study of the problem can finally inspire a solution which will comply with your wishes, and the demands of the inspectors.

Remember that the official requirements as to ceiling heights, ventilation and so on can often have very adverse effects on the external appearance of a building. Seek relaxation of the regulations, if necessary, since local authorities have powers to do this when dealing with works under certain sections. Notable exceptions are parts D and E regarding structural stability and fire respectively. Even under these headings you will find that there are far more ways than you might at first imagine of meeting the statutory requirements.

Finally, do not be persuaded that because an extension carried out in some fashionable modern idiom is 'honest' it will therefore necessarily be successful. Beauty may owe much to artifice, and your objectives should be aesthetic rather than moral ones. The work should triumph or fail on that basis. The sad fact is that wicked men may promote great art as readily as good ones may engender ugliness.

GLOSSARY

AGGREGATE: Stones, chippings, gravel, clinker, etc., used to give bulk and strength to a mix of concrete.

ARCH (FOUR-CENTRED): The most flattened -out version of the pointed arch, so called because its design is set out by centering a pair of compasses at four different positions.

ARCHITRAVE: A moulding in wood or plaster around the sides and head of a door or window opening. It also serves to decorate and cover the joint between the wall surface and frame.

ASBESTOS-CEMENT SLATES: Blue-black imitations of machine-cut Welsh slate (usually 12 ins x 24 ins) composed of asbestos fibres and cement.

ASHLAR: Accurately cut facing stone, constructed with very fine joints.

BALUSTERS: Vertical supports in stone, metal or wood supporting a staircase hand-rail, landing balustrade or external balustrade capping.

BAY WINDOW: Window protruding from the main wall of a building, having its own side walls and roof. It does not curve like a bow window. The structure must rise from ground level, unlike an oriel.

BONDER OR BONDING TIMBER: Timbers built length-ways into the thickness of old stone or brick walls to provide additional strength to the wall and bearings for joists. They usually rot and cause severe problems.

'BOTTLE GLASS': Window panes given this name are really pieces of blown glass discs, where they have been broken off from the blow pipe during manufacture, leaving a 'bullion'. See Crown Glass. Also called 'Bull's Eye Panes'.

BOW WINDOW: A late 18th and early 19th century curved window, especially favoured for shops and taverns. (see Fig 25)

BUILDING REGULATIONS: Statutory regulations (of some complexity), which oblige those carrying out various types of building work to apply for consent from the Local Authority, subject plans and have the works inspected. Pay great attention to these.

CASEMENT WINDOW: A side-hinged window. In England these open outwards. (see Fig. 17)

CESS-PIT: Large, underground, water-proof storage tank, into which drains are run. Tank must be pumped out at regular intervals.

CLADDING: Weather-proofing and/or decorative surfaces, fixed to the structural elements of a wall, i.e. slates, tiles, weather boards, etc.

COLLARS: Horizontal timbers, spiked to each pair of rafters, checking any tendency for the ends of the rafters to pull apart under load. Attic ceilings are often fixed to these.

COMPOSITION CONCRETE TILES: Roofing tiles made from a type of close-textured concrete, usually coloured, and sometimes intended to imitate a natural stone. Some are in in plain tile form, but many are interlocking.

CONCRETE: Mixture of cement, sand and other aggregates in such proportions as 1:2:4.

CONSOLE: A type of timber, stone or plaster bracket, usually in the form of an 'S' scroll, sometimes called 'ancones'. (Fig 76)

COPING: A course of fairly substantial stones which usually top a parapet or upstanding gable walls.

CORNICE: The top-most element in a classical entablature. The term is applied to moulded features over doors, under the eaves of roofs and around the ceilings of rooms.

COURSES: Bricks, stones, concrete blocks, etc, are laid row upon row in 'courses'.

CORBEL: A stone or timber support, which projects from a wall to carry the load of a structural member such as a beam. It may sometimes serve a purely decorative function.

COVE: A simple and fairly substantial concave moulding, usually found at the intersection of ceilings and walls, and along the eaves of early 18th century houses.

CROSS-BATTEN: A wooden batten laid across pieces of boarding and nailed to hold them together. Much the same as a 'ledge'

CROWN GLASS: As late as the 1830's, glass was still being manufactured by the crown glass method. This involved blowing a glass disc from which a number of rectangular window panes could then be cut. A pane cut from the part of the disc attached to the blow pipe bears a distinctive circular whorl called a bullion.

BARGE-BOARDS: Boards, sometimes of ornamental design, which run down the verges of a gabled roof, concealing and protecting the ends of the roof timbers.

BEAMS: Timbers of relatively large cross-sectional area, which span between walls, pillars or piers and normally support joists.

DAMP-PROOF COURSE: A layer of impervious material, built into the thickness of a wall to prevent moisture rising from the ground into the main structure.

DAMP-PROOF MEMBRANE: Normally a layer of plastic sheeting, laid over the site hardcore of a modern building, to prevent moisture rising from the ground into the floor structure. Also used in restoration work for damp-proofing.

DOOR HOOD: A projecting feature, usually supported on brackets, which gives visual emphasis to a doorway, and may also serve to keep the weather off those seeking admission.

DORMER WINDOW: A window which protrudes from the slope of a roof, having its own miniature roofing structure, and sides called 'cheeks'.

ENTABLATURE: The topmost horizontal element of a classical order of architecture. Consists of a cornice, frieze and architrave - reading downwards.

FASCIA BOARD: The board which runs horizontally under the eaves of a building, to which the guttering is normally attached.

FEATHER-EDGED BOARDING: Plain weather-boards, tapering in thickness, so that the thick bottom edge of one overlaps the thin top edge of the one below. Old types had a rough, sawn finish. (Fig 32)

FLASHINGS: Strips of water-proof material (usually lead), used to weather the abutments between slates and chimneys; walls and roofs; walls and windows, etc.

FRENCH WINDOWS: Pairs of narrow, glazed doors giving access to the outside. They open inwards, as do ordinary windows in France, from which their name derives.

GLAZING BARS: Wooden framing members in a window sash which divide and contain the glass panes. Early bars (late 17th C. and Queen Anne) were wide, flat and rather crudely designed. They became progressively thinner, and often more subtly moulded in the 18th century. Early 19th century bars were very thin indeed.

HOOD MOULDING: A moulding usually seen over the top of early window openings (see Fig 15)

HOPPER HEAD: Sometimes called a 'bucket head', this is part of a rainwater system which gathers water from various pipes into a downpipe.

HORNS: Sash horns are continuations of the sash stiles, making it possible to form the joint between stile and rail with a mortice and tenon. A Victorian feature. (see Fig 4)

INTERLOCKING TILES: These, unlike plain tiles, are designed so that their edges fit mechanically one with another, to provide a weather seal. (Fig 49)

JAMBS: The vertical sides of a wall opening, i.e. window jambs, door jambs and fireplace jambs.

JOISTS: Horizontal timbers (normally placed on edge), which structurally support floor boards and flat roof deckings.

KEYSTONE: The centre stone of an arch, against which the other stones (voussoirs) are butted. Applies also to brick arches.

LAUNDERS: The Cornish term for gutters.

LATTICE WINDOW PANE: A casement window normally glazed with diamond-shaped panes set in lead cames.

LINTEL: A member, usually of stone, timber or concrete, which carries the structural load over a door, window or fireplace opening.

LEDGED AND BRACED DOOR: A simple door formed of vertical boards held together by wooden 'ledges' nailed across them. A diagonal 'brace' is nailed between the ledges, and is sometimes housed into them to prevent the door dropping at the edge furthest from the hinges. (Fig 69)

LATH AND PLASTER: Plaster of various types of composition is applied to a 'key' of thin, wooden laths which are nailed to a timber framework for walls and ceilings.

MODILLIONS: Console brackets fitted beneath the overhang of a cornice as a form of decoration.

MORTAR: Normally a mixture of cement and sand; but may include lime as well, or be composed of lime and sand only.

MOULDINGS: Shaped lengths of great variety in plaster, stone or wood, used as ornament, weathering and for the concealment of joints between one building surface and another. (see Fig 15) and 'Cornices'.

MULLIONS: Stone or timber uprights, dividing window openings *vertically* into separate 'lights' (see Fig 15)

MULLION AND TRANSOM WINDOW: See Fig 11 (old) and Fig 19 (modern).

NEWEL: Structural post in stone, metal or wood, supporting a balustrade at the top, bottom and changes of direction in a staircase.

NOGGING: Short timbers which strut the gaps between studs (see studding). Also 'brick nogging' used to fill the panels of timber-framed buildings.

NORFOLK AND SUFFOLK LATCHES: Latches consisting of a simple handgrip and thumbplate on one side of the door, and a wooden or metal sneck on the other. (see Fig 72)

ORDERS OF ARCHITECTURE: The formal compositions of columns and entablatures in classical Greek and Roman architecture. The main orders are: Doric, Tuscan, Ionic, Corinthian and Composite. Most architectural books show these in detail.

PEBBLE DASH: Wall rendering, liberally covered with fairly small, smooth pebbles, while the mortar is still soft.

PEDIMENT: A triangular (sometimes segmental) feature, usually of timber, stone or plaster, which forms the topmost element of a classical door or window. (see Fig 51)

PITCH (of a roof): The angle at which the slope of a roof lies to the horizontal. (see Fig 47)

PLANNING PERMISSION: Statutory permission which must be obtained from a local authority when various types of new building and development are proposed. Other aspects involving this permission are change of use of property, and work which may affect 'listed' buildings, or buildings in 'conservation areas'. Be very careful to find out from experts whether this permission is required.

POINTING: The visible mortar filling between bricks or stones in a wall.

POLLARDING: Process of cutting the whole top off a tree, severing right through the trunk. Method promotes growth of numerous new shoots, but can be very ugly.

PRINCIPAL RAFTERS: The heavy, main rafters which carry the whole roof-load, consisting of purlins, common rafters, battens and slates, in a double roof.

PURLINS: Normally square-section timbers, running lengthways along the roof, and resting on the principal rafters. Purlins carry the lighter and more numerous common rafters.

QUOINS: Squared-up or 'dressed' stones, which form the corners of a building.

RAFTERS: Main structural timbers upon which a pitched roof is laid.

RAILS: Horizontal members in various kinds of timber framing of doors, windows and panelling.

REINFORCED CONCRETE: Concrete, containing steel bars, which greatly increase its strength.

RENDERING: A layer of plaster, mortar, etc, used to cover a wall or similar surface.

REVEAL: The outside part of a window jamb between the main wall surface and the window frame.

RIBBON OR STRAP POINTING: Pointing between stones which protrudes beyond the face of the stone, forming a ribbon-like pattern of mortar. (see Fig 39)

RIDGE: The apex of a pitched roof where one slope meets the other.

RIDGE BOARD AND RIDGE POLE: Timber running along the apex of the roof. Ridge board is sandwiched between the tops of the rafters. Ridge pole is cradled by the ends of the rafters in various ways.

RIDGE TILE: Angled, or half-round tile used to weather the junction between the roof slope coverings at the ridge.

ROOF TRUSSES: Pairs of rafters, tied by a third member, to form a load-bearing triangle of timber or steel.

ROUGH CAST: Wall rendering onto which a mixture of lime and aggregate has been thrown before setting. Ugly, modern versions contain cement and may be thrown by mechanical means (Tyrolean finish).

SASH: The glazed part of a window. It will normally open. Usually suspended rather than hinged.

SASH-FRAME: The frame in which the sashes are suspended, fixed or hinged. Includes: stiles, head and sill.

SASH BOX: The upright part of a double-hung sash window frame, in which the sash weights are suspended.

SASH WINDOW (Double-hung): Window with suspended sashes, opened and closed by vertical movement. (see Fig 8)

SASH WINDOW (Sliding): Window with sash, or sashes, which open and close by sliding horizontally within the frame. (Figs 12 & 13)

SCREED: Usually a fairly thin (say 2") layer of mortar laid and levelled as a floor surface, upon which tiles and other finishes may be placed.
SILL: The external window member of wood, slate, stone, brick or concrete which aids rainwater in running off the window and clear of the wall face.
SOFFIT: The underneath surface of lintels, window openings, beams, stairs and roof eaves, etc.
SPATTER-DASH: Rough rendering for walls, applied by flicking lumps of soft plaster onto the wall (see Fig 38)
SPLAY: The jambs of a window or door opening are called splays, if they open out at an angle.
STRAP HINGES: Also known as cross-garnets, these consist of a flat, wrought iron bar, curled over at one end to form a socket. This fits over an iron pin attached to the door jamb. (see Fig 73)
STRUT: A timber (or steel) member which braces two structural building components apart, i.e. between floor joists.
STRING COURSE: A band of projecting masonry, brick or plaster, often at or around first floor sill level, having a mainly decorative purpose. (Fig 78)
STUCCO: A form of smooth and relatively hard rendering, much favoured for the walls of early 19th century and Victorian houses.
STUDDING: Upright timbers of sizes such as 4" x 2", which form the main framework of such units as walls and partitions.
STILES: Upright members in various kinds of timber framing of doors and windows.
SEPTIC TANK: A sealed waterproof tank, usually below ground, in which waste material from a drainage system is biologically decomposed, before finally being part-purified and dispersed through a soakaway. The latter is often constructed in conjunction with the tank.
STEEL TROWEL FINISH: Smooth finish for walls and floor screeds, carried out with a steel plasterer's trowel. (see Fig 34)
TEXTURED PAINTS: Paints and similar solutions containing various types of fine, granular material to give texture.
TILE (Clay): Baked earthenware roofing and floor units, not to be confused with a slate which is a natural stone, riven and cut to various sizes. (see Fig 49)
THROATING: A groove along the underside of a component such as a sill, to form a drip for moisture trying to run back into the wall face.
TONGUE AND GROOVE BOARDING: Floor boards are typical. The protruding edge of one fits into a slot in the edge of the next.
TOPPINGS: Mixture of small stones and fine grit etc, used by road contractors to consolidate hardcore.
TRANSOM: Stone or timber members which divide window openings *horizontally* into separate lights. (see Fig 11)
TYROLEAN FINISH: Wall finish, applied by spraying a mixture of plaster grout and fine sharp stone chippings. This is done with a special hand-operated spraying machine.
VERGES: The exposed ends of a sloping roof, where the slates or tiles overhang the gable walls.
VERNACULAR BUILDING: Everyday buildings, usually of indigenous local style.
VERTICAL CRAZY PAVING: Unevenly shaped and relatively thin slabs of stone, applied with mortar to a wall surface.
VOUSSOIRS: Specially cut stones of wedge-shape, which make up the structure or facing of an arch.
WALL PLATE: Length of timber, which runs along the top of a wall to provide a bearing and fixing for the ends of rafters.
WANEY-EDGE WEATHERBOARD: Weatherboards having a wavy outline along the bottom edge of each board, giving a vaguely rustic appearance. (see Fig 42)
WINDOW BOARD: The board inside a window which most people call a window sill.
WOOD FLOAT: A plastering tool, consisting of a flat piece of wood, with a handle for texturing renderings before they set. (Fig 34)

THE AUTHOR

The writer has always been interested in old buildings and lives in a once derelict Cornish farmhouse which he converted himself.

After leaving Marlborough College, he trained as a journalist, working on a provincial evening newspaper as a reporter. He subsequently worked in London as assistant editor of a magazine in a well-known publishing group and later in public relations.

After moving to the West Country, from which his father's family originates, he qualified in building construction, becoming a Licentiate of the Institute of Building. He now practices as a consultant, specialising in matters connected with old houses. He is also a lecturer in further education on old buildings and their contents, architecture and interior design.

Economics now dictate that many people plan and even carry out their own conversion and repair work. The writer hopes that this booklet will be a useful guide to retaining the character of their houses and cottages. Illustrated with more than 70 photographs and drawings, it aims to put forward the aesthetic aspects in a practical way.